CHILD ART
WITH EVERYDAY MATERIALS

Tarit Bhattacharjee

Written by
Kanchana Arni
and
Gita Wolf

Tara Publishing

The School in Madras is one of seven Krishnamurti Foundation schools in India. We are most happy that Gita Wolf and Kanchana Arni have documented *Child Art with Everyday Materials,* based on their conversations with our art teacher Tarit Bhattacharjee, and their observation of the work in our art room. We would like to express our gratitude for their great effort bringing to light an important dimension of our school's work in such a readable and aesthetic form. We hope that teachers and parents would find here something that permits them to share an artistic and creative relationship with children.

G. Gautama   June 1996
Principal, The School, Madras
Krishnamurthi Foundation India

CREATIVITY WITHOUT BARRIERS

This book explores the philosophy and practice of children's art, which I have developed as a teacher at The School, Krishnamurthi Foundation India, Madras. The works reproduced here were created by my students.

My approach cannot be called a professional art course. That is not my aim. I teach about 300 children every year, and I have taught for the last 10 years. Hardly any of my students have become professional artists. What, then, is the basis of my art teaching?

The challenge has been to provide a creative environment through art. A creative person is never bored, and he is able to draw strength and sustenance from his own imaginative activity. A strong creative foundation is necessary for children to develop into mature, thinking adults.

My work with children must be viewed in the context of the educational philosophy of our school. We encourage activities which bring in global consciousness and environmental awareness. Our ethos emphasizes originality and independent thinking. Questioning the influence of the media is also part of our agenda. We do not encourage comparison—there are no art competitions. At the same time, there is an emphasis on the simple and natural. Art is integral to our education—it has an important role in academic as well as non-academic fields.

Over the years, it is the creative freedom provided by the school which has allowed me to develop my approach. There have been absolutely no constraints or demands on me as an art teacher.

It is my belief that art is essential in any child's—or adult's—life. In the context of contemporary life and rigidly structured education, art offers perhaps the only space for individual vision. It is part of self-affirmation. There are no right or wrong answers, no judgements possible. You are free to express your own unique vision and explore your own creativity. This, to me, is the reason art needs a more central position in education.

So, in my art classes, there is no pressure to produce, perform, or finish work quickly. The atmosphere is relaxed, playful, and at times very chaotic. Children are not expected to paint portraits or landscapes. They do not systematically try out the different media. Their exposure to abstract concepts like perspective is limited. Occasionally, we talk about folk art, or look at the works of great artists. But not for too long. Children begin to get bored, or despair of measuring up to Leonardo da Vinci. Comparison and imitation dry up creativity.

The art I teach has essentially evolved from observing children, as well as from the folk traditions I experienced during my own childhood. I find it more challenging to evolve art from the point of view of the child, rather than attempt to mould him to abstract concepts. In a sense, children have taught me art. They are spontaneous, restless, playful, and enjoy making a mess. They love random surprise effects. They are naturally experimental and observant. Their work is fresh, innocent and fearless in tackling any theme. Children want to depict reality in their art. They do not intend to be abstract. They depict reality just as they see it. This directness is not caught up with problems of technique, style or innovation, and is very close to some forms of folk art.

Children get frustrated easily when their work does not measure up to their own expectations. It is, therefore, important not to set any standards. I do not want children to struggle. I do not want to add to the burden of an already pressurized child. There should be no stress, tension, competition, or even fear of competition. Art should not lead to frustration or rejection. It is much too positive. *Basically, art has no rules whatsoever.* To acknowledge this is to experience freedom. My classes are, therefore, experimental, rather than structured.

Having said that, it is also true that my own vision is not part of any school of thought. I use different approaches for each individual, and as an art teacher, I have a chance to get to know the personality of each of my students. In the case of a quiet, shy child, I might ask him to sit under a tree, observe details quietly, and work slowly, with attention. A restless child will

need outlets which will allow her to use bold strokes and quick techniques. Sometimes, the process can even be reversed. The main thing is to recognize the child's capabilities and to structure projects accordingly. Every individual wants to express something. Restless and even violent children can relax and enjoy themselves.

In a way, I conceive of art as therapy. Children these days are influenced by television and the media. There is violence everywhere. There is no way of ignoring or restricting these influences. The art room can be a place where creativity can emerge from chaos and ugliness. Once, while working with a group, I noticed five boys modelling swords, knives and guns. I let them be. After sometime, I asked them whether they could 'see' any other forms in their work. One child slowly put in the features of a face, and a mask emerged.

The other influence of media is stereotyping. I get children who want to copy Mickey Mouse endlessly. I try to tell them that this is somebody else's image — what about their own version? We have rich visual traditions in folk, tribal and primitive art. We can draw on these for inspiration, instead of looking to homogenized, stereotypical media images.

The significance of folk traditions lies in their expressive use of simple every-day materials to create art. The importance of this for today's privileged child cannot be overemphasized. Simple resources are no longer valued these days. Art materials tend to be ready-made and expensive. Why do we need this at all? Art does not require a lot of sophisticated materials. One way of inculcating respect for simple resources is to look around you, use what is available, and recycle as much as possible. *Art must emerge from the materials on hand.* This approach stimulates the child to observe her surroundings long after the art session is over, and to think of creative uses for things she picks up. While this is the basis of my art education, I do have some guidelines on which I base practical sessions.

I try to consciously break some forms of conditioning, like the use of clean white paper to begin art. I do not encourage instruments like compasses, rulers, or even erasers. The accidental and spontaneous are very valuable. There is also a great need to overcome the stumbling block of "I can't draw." Even those who do not enjoy drawing or painting can create wonderful art. Another thing I have a problem with is the strict division between 'art' and 'craft.' Some of these concerns are evident in this book.

It has been broadly structured according to a conceptual framework, yet these examples of the work I have done with children defy final classification. Neither are they graded according to age levels. They testify to the fact that anyone can do any kind of art with anything.

In the final analysis, art cannot be taught. It evolves from exposure, activity and experience. An art educator can only provide some guidance which sparks off the inner creativity present in each one of us. Perhaps this book can do that for you.

Tarit Bhattacharjee
In conversation with Kanchana Arni and Gita Wolf
February 1996

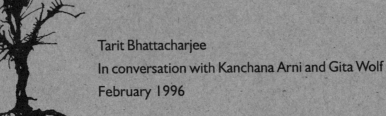

BETWEEN PHILOSOPHY AND PRACTICE: WHAT THIS BOOK IS ABOUT

When we first entered Tarit's art room, we were overwhelmed by the striking work strewn all over. How had children created such extraordinary art?

This became a quest over the next year, which finally lead to the making of this book. We sat in on Tarit's classes, and had endless discussions with him. We observed and recorded work sessions. From conventional art backgrounds ourselves, his unique approach was new and exciting. It opened up a world of creativity without barriers.

His perspective was holistic, combining vision with practicality. Art was no longer about copying the outlines of a horse or colouring an apple red. It was not concerned with depicting a theme. It did not require particular skills or expensive materials. It had no rules at all. And though the approach was developed in the context of an alternative vision of school education, it was universally applicable. Creativity has a place in everyone's lives.

As we went on, the child in each of us surfaced, and we found ourselves eager to try out Tarit's methods. Soon, we began evolving our own exercises and enjoying ourselves thoroughly. How could this rich experience be made accessible to others?

It took us over a year to work through our material and arrive at a way of presenting it. To systematize, without losing complexity, was the most difficult task. The categories obviously flow into each other. Broadly, we have tried to maintain a balance between philosophy and practice, without sacrificing simplicity or directness.

The book works in different ways:

- It can serve as a manual for art educators at all levels. At the same time, it documents an alternative educational perspective.

- It can also be an activity book for children and adults, to experiment with art. Children who use this book on their own may like to go straight to the exercises. We have kept the instructions simple, but it goes without saying that they need not be followed exactly. The possibilities and variations are endless. Younger children can try out simple versions of an exercise, while older ones may like to experiment further.

- By exploring some abstract concepts, we also hope to offer insights into ways of developing one's own creative vision.

- Finally, this is a tribute to child art, a unique collection which documents the creative power inherent in all children.

The art in this book is entitled to appreciation in its own right. At the same time, we would like to invite you to try it yourselves. Everybody can create art.

Gita Wolf
Kanchana Arni   February 1996

We are grateful to The School, Krishnamurthi Foundation India, Madras, for their generous support throughout this project, and for permission to reproduce the art created by students of the school. Ours is more than a formal acknowledgment. We became acquainted, at first hand, with educational approaches which were serious, as well as playful. We appreciate not only the informal access to art classes, but also the chance to enjoy the warmth and creativity characteristic of the school. This was a large part of the joy this project brought us.

Contents

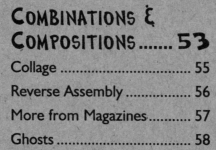

LINES & DESIGNS

Lines are all around us—from alphabets to measurements. Line is also a basic element in art. It defines a space and turns it into composition. Lines start from a dot on a page, and go on to intricate drawings.

All children naturally play with line—they scribble on walls and trace patterns on dust.

Design is an integral part of our daily social life. In rural India, women draw patterns with rice flour in the yards outside their houses. Folk and tribal art styles also use ornamentation and design in unique ways.

These traditions have inspired a means of exploring design in art. This helps to plan, choose and arrange compositions based on design and ornamentation.

Outlines: Hand and Foot

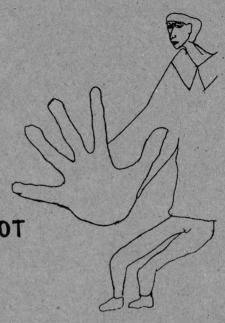

Materials

White paper, felt pens or crayons.

- Place your hand on the white paper, palm facing downwards.

- Outline your hand with a felt pen.

- Look at the spaces created within and around the outline.

- How can you develop them?

Variations

- Try an outline of your foot.

- You can even lie down on a large sheet of paper and get a friend to trace your outline. How can this be developed into a picture?

- Think of other objects—like ice cream sticks, spoons, or cartons—you can trace. You could place the object in different positions or combine the outlines of different objects to create interesting effects.

- Try outlining with jagged or uneven lines.

LINES CHANGE SHAPES

Sometimes it is hard to start art work. Random shapes evoke associations. Lines can transform these associations into art.

Materials

Newspaper, glue, white paper, paint, brushes.

* Tear up newspaper into random shapes.

* Glue these shapes on a sheet of white paper.

* What do these shapes suggest? What can they be turned into?

* Outline these shapes with black poster paint.

* Add designs to complete the picture.

Variation

* Use magazine, brown or coloured paper.

Colour First

Children usually draw figures and colour them in. To focus attention on the quality of line—its ability to define shapes—reverse the approach to drawing and painting. Colour first, and then add lines to make a picture.

Materials

White paper, crayons, black felt pen.

- Using the flat side of a small piece of crayon, colour a shape—it could be a human figure, a dinosaur, a tree, a bird, an animal, or a house.

- Outline your drawing with a black felt pen.

Variation

- Try effects with a fuzzy outline.

BUILDING BLOCKS

Here is a simple way to enable even a small child to begin a composition, and to use the concept of design as a tool for creative expression.

Materials

Paper, pencil/paints, brushes.

♦ Just as you need materials like sand, cement, bricks, tiles or wood to build a house, a picture can also be built up of elements.

♦ Create a store of design elements like

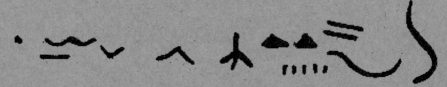

♦ Choose one element, say a dot, and use it in different ways on a sheet of paper.

♦ Continue, by using the other elements in your store. This can be done in any fashion you choose.

♦ Once you have created a number of designs on the page, pause and observe. Can these elements be formed into a composition?

♦ Do these shapes suggest something? Is one section of the design interesting? Can it be enlarged, coloured or used in a particular way?

COLOURS

Art work need not begin with a clean white sheet of paper on which bright colour is applied. Folk art, for example, uses earth colours on textured backgrounds. Colour works in different ways. Very young children enjoy using bright primary colours. Exposure to the subtler aspects of shades and tones develops aesthetic sensitivity and maturity.

Monotones

You can get shades and tones by using only one colour.

Materials

White paper, black poster paint, brushes, water.

* Paint a picture in black outline.

* Fill in details using black paint diluted with different amounts of water.

* Use decorative elements like dots, dashes, and lines.

* How many shades do you see? What effects do the tones and shades produce?

BLACKOUTS

Materials

Newspaper, cellotape, oil, black poster paint, brushes, water.

* Cut strips of cellotape and glue them on to the paper. This can be done in either a planned or random fashion.

* Dab oil on the paper.

* Dip the paper in diluted black paint and allow it to dry.

* Carefully remove the cellotape.

* Look at the composition in different tones. How can it be developed?

* Complete the picture with black paint.

Variation

* Try this exercise with different colours.

FLOWER POWER

You do not need commercial colours to paint a picture. Crushing leaves, flowers and vegetables is a simple way of making vegetable dyes. These colours are mellow, giving a subdued effect which is not possible with bright chemical paints. It opens up a new world of colour which is subtle and gentle.

Materials

Flowers, leaves, charcoal, tea, beetroot or other coloured vegetables, white paper.

* Colour the paper with tea. You can even allow the tea to drip onto the paper.

* Crush the leaves, flowers and vegetables, and directly rub them on the paper.

* What forms can you see?

* Outline your forms in charcoal and add details.

Brown
Make strong tea.
Strain and use.

Green
Cut up leaves and boil in water.

Terracotta
Rub a piece of brick and dilute with water.

Yellow
Mix turmeric powder with water.

Orange
Dilute tomato ketchup with water.

Pink
Boil beetroot in water.

Thickener
Boil sago, stirring until thick. Cool and use as a thickener for all colours.

BACKGROUND EXPERIMENTS

Colour works differently
on different backgrounds.
Experiment with dark or
black backgrounds.

SHAPES & SPACES

Cutting out and tearing paper is the best way to understand two dimensional shapes. Geometric shapes are basic and clear. An understanding of the way these basic shapes work together can develop a sense of composition.

Space is not limited to canvas or paper. Art can be created on large spaces, like the painted walls of village homes. Or it can be finely worked out within a small space, like miniatures. Reflect on how best a given space can be used, not merely fill up available area. The space you choose to work on determines the nature of the work.

CUT OUTS

Materials

Black paper, white paper, scissors, glue.

- Cut out shapes in black paper.

- Decorate the shapes further by folding and cutting in to them.

- Glue these shapes on white paper.

- What do they suggest? Can more features and details be added? How can the basic shapes be developed further?

Variations

- Try outlining the shapes with plain or jagged lines.

- Try using newspaper or different coloured papers.

- Try tearing instead of cutting shapes.

- The paper need not necessarily be bright. Try combining shapes cut out of brown, black, or newspaper.

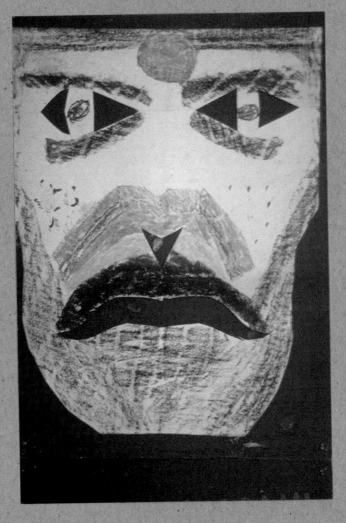

MASKS

Materials

Coloured paper, white paper, felt pens, glue, scissors.

- Cut out the outline of a face on white paper.

- Fold the paper in half, and cut out shapes for eyes, nose, and mouth.

- Glue the mask on to a coloured background.

- Outline the cut-out features of the mask with felt pens, so that the shape stands out.

Variations

- Raise the contours of a cut-out mask slightly, and glue the edges on a sheet of paper to create a three-dimensional effect.

- Try making animal masks.

Doing Something Big

Materials

Four sheets of brown paper, powder or poster paints, brushes, glue.

- Glue the overlapping edges of four sheets of brown paper to form a large background.

- Look at the background. How can the spaces be used best? Which spaces look empty? Which need to be left empty?

- Think of simple, large figures or objects to put in, keeping in mind the space available.

- Once you have outlined your figures, work out the rest of your composition, on the same scale.

- How is it different from usual compositions? How did you use your brush?

We decided to draw a boat with people, using earth colours.

27

MINIATURES

Like outsize pictures, miniatures also allow you to experiment with spaces.

Materials

Old visiting cards, black felt pen, white paper, poster paints.

* Draw small pictures or scenes on each visiting card.

* Arrange them on the white paper background—either randomly, or in a pattern.

* Move them around, until you are happy with the composition, and then glue them on to the white paper.

* Outline each of the cards with a black felt pen.

* Colour the remaining spaces in the background, adding designs if you like.

Variations

* Instead of painting the background, try using coloured paper.

* You can also draw miniatures directly on the background instead of using visiting cards.

* Create interesting miniatures out of triangles or circles.

VERTICAL AND HORIZONTAL SPACES

A picture does not need to be within a rectangle. A long vertical or horizontal strip of paper breaks this convention and suggests interesting possibilities for compositions.

Materials

Long, rectangular sheet of brown paper, crayons, water colours, brushes.

* Look at the strip of paper—do you want to use it horizontally or vertically?

* What kinds of associations do you have with vertical space? A tree? A building?

* What about horizontal spaces? A river? A road?

* Outline your composition with black paint.

* Fill in details using crayons and water colours.

Variation

* Try combining vertical and horizontal spaces and working on them.

Narrative Scrolls

In many folk traditions of India, singers and storytellers narrate their tales with the help of a long painted scroll. This 'illustrates' their narrative. Scrolls are a wonderful way of painting and telling a story. They use visual space uniquely.

Materials

Newspaper, black paper, poster paints, brushes, scissors, glue.

* Think of a story, song or rhyme you would like to illustrate.

* Cut the newspaper into rectangles or squares.

* Paint successive scenes from your story on the newspaper panels.

* Cut and glue the black paper into a strip long enough to fit in all the newspaper panels.

* Glue the panels successively on to the black paper scroll.

* The scroll can be operated horizontally or vertically, by unrolling it scene by scene, as the story unfolds.

Variation

* Try a scroll which is painted continuously and not separated into panels.

TEXTURES & IMPRESSIONS

The walls of many homes in rural India are plastered with mud. People then paint and decorate them. This simple and striking art form is the basis for experiments with textures and impressions.

Try working with textures and impressions created by everyday materials like leaves, sticks, or bottle caps. It activates observation skills, and makes you look for materials which can create interesting textures.

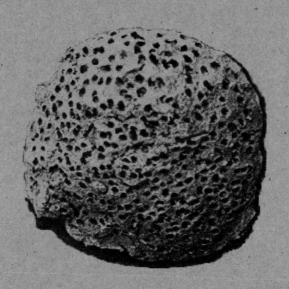

Texture Trials

Children love taking impressions from things. Clay is a good medium to experiment with textures.

Materials

Clay, a stick or piece of bark.

- Make a slab of clay. It should not be too sticky.

- Press a stick or a piece of bark on it.

- Remove, and look at the impression created.

Variation

- Try textures with other materials: a piece of jute, net, combs, forks, bottle caps . . .

- Develop the textures in to an animal or human face.

C. DEEPTI + KRISHNAPRIYA

PAINT ON WALLS

During a clay project, some clay stuck to the newspapers we had laid out to protect the floor. These looked like mud walls of village homes. This led to an exploration of texture.

Materials

Newspaper, mud or chalk powder, paints, brushes.

* Make a paste of mud and water, or chalk and water.

* Smear it on a sheet of newspaper and allow it to dry.

* The paper will take on an interesting texture. The newsprint can show through. This will create unusual effects. This surface can now be used for painting.

* You can use paints, powder colours, or experiment with making your own vegetable dyes with crushed leaves.

* Observe how the newspaper script and the texture can be used to compose the work.

* Earthy colours like black, white, ochre, and green work particularly well on mud texture.

STICK IN THE MUD

People in ancient times depicted stories and scenes from their lives in cave paintings. The simplicity of their materials inspired this experiment.

Materials

Newspaper, diluted clay, stick, brushes, powdered charcoal, white paint.

- Apply diluted clay on a sheet of newspaper.

- Using a stick, make outlines of figures, houses, trees, or animals.

- Wait for this to dry.

- Brush on powdered charcoal with a dry brush on some of the areas.

- Outline with white paint.

Changing Patterns

Art need not be permanent. It is an experience where the joy of creating is most important. Small children love tracing designs on sand. It is a wonderful way to feel material.

Materials

Sand, newspaper.

* Spread a thin layer of sand on a newspaper.

* Trace out designs and shapes with your fingers.

* You can even fill in the lines and spaces with powder colour.

Variation

* Outline any shape with black paint. Apply a layer of glue within it. Sprinkle sand evenly over the glue.

Rainy Day

On a rainy day, a child who couldn't think of any other subject, went out to look at the rain, and drew an umbrella. That formed the stencil for this print of a rainy day. Such textures can be created by simple printing techniques.

Materials

Black printing ink, piece of plywood or hardboard, two sheets of white paper, scissors, rolling pin or smooth bottle.

- Draw a shape on a piece of white paper.

- Cut it out. This is a stencil.

- Cover the surface of the wood or board with black printing ink and place the stencil over it.

- Cover the stencil and the inked background with a clean sheet of white paper.

- Roll over the paper with a rolling pin or smooth bottle to get an impression.

Variation

- Roll ink on a sheet of paper. Then cut out a shape.

- What else can you use instead of a roller? What about a pencil or a blunt stick? Think of other ways to create interesting effects.

LEAF IMPRESSIONS

This session evolved from a child who rolled a bottle with paint on it. The 'mess' she made resulted in some very interesting textures.

Materials

White paper, black printing ink, water colour, brushes, some leaves with well defined veins, rolling pin or smooth bottle.

- Look at the leaf carefully. Normally, the underside of the leaf has more prominent veins.

- Lay the leaf on the table with the veins facing upwards.

- Apply ink on a rolling pin or smooth bottle and roll this over the leaf, so that some of the ink coats the leaf surface.

- Place a white sheet of paper on the table.

- Carefully place the leaf on the paper with the ink side down.

- Clean the roller and roll it over the leaf so the impression gets transferred on the paper.

Variation

- What effects can you achieve if you use your hands or a ruler instead of the roller?

- Can you compose a picture with leaf prints? How can the composition be linked? With outlines and paint?

Two men made from leaf prints.

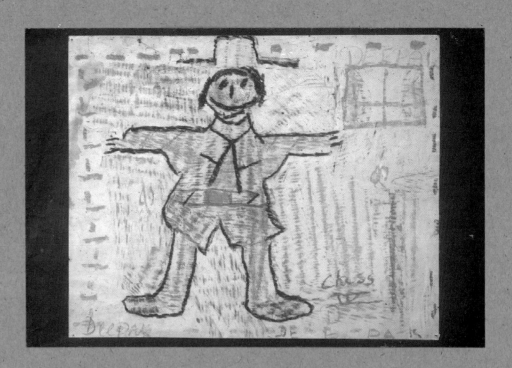

MAT PRINTS

This experiment was inspired by coin rubbing, which all children enjoy.

Materials

Straw mat, white paper, crayons.

◆ Place a white sheet of paper over the mat.

◆ Hold the paper down firmly with one hand and rub the broad side of the crayon over it.

◆ Remove the paper from the mat and look at the texture created. What does it suggest?

◆ Outline the forms you want with black crayon.

Variation

◆ Experiment with other surfaces to create textures: bamboo, cane, corrugated cardboard, tree bark, embossed leather, carved surfaces, badges ...

◆ Try combining textures.

FORMS

Form is the way a work is put together. Forms are all around us. Three-dimensional forms can best be grasped through a material like clay. It can dry out naturally, if there is no facility for firing it. Clay allows you to create a form, feel it and change it. Children love the feel of clay in their hands. See how it feels—handle it and play with it!

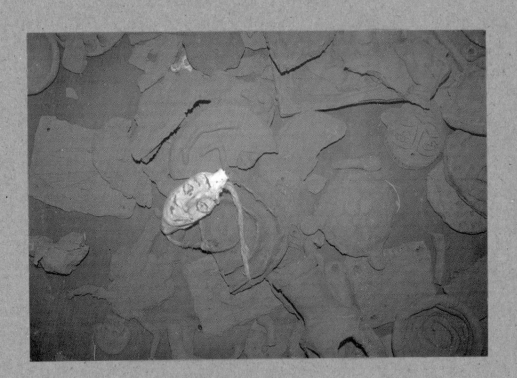

COILS

Children naturally tend to fashion long coils, like snakes, with clay. Coils are the easiest way of forming clay. They can be used as building blocks for objects or sculptures.

Materials

Clay.

- Form a ball with clay.
- Roll out the ball with the palm of your hand into a long rope or 'snake'.
- Form the rope into a flat coil.

Variation

- Create a pot with coils.
- Try making jewellery with small coils.

TILES

Making flat objects, like tiles, is a good way to understand form. Adding a few raised elements introduces the child to the concept of three-dimensional sculpture.

Materials

Clay, rolling pin

- Using a rolling pin, or the palm of your hand, make a slab of clay.
- What does the shape of the 'tile' suggest?
- Add features like eyes, eyebrows, nose, and mouth with coils of clay.

Variation

- Try scooping out the features instead of adding them.
- Experiment with different shapes of tiles.

CYLINDERS

Strong enough to be used in sculpture, a hollow cylinder allows creative exploration of inner and outer spaces.

Materials

Clay, ruler.

- Form a ball with clay.

- Roll it into a thick solid cylinder using your palm.

- Cut the cylinder into two.

- Place one cylinder on the table, and using the edge of your palm, flatten it out gently and evenly. Now it is a rectangle.

- Flatten the other cylinder in the same way.

- Join both rectangles with their longer sides together, to form a large rectangle.

- Bring together the outer edges to make a hollow cylinder.

- With the help of the flat side of a ruler, smoothen the surface and top edge of the clay cylinder.

- Create cylinders of various sizes. They can be the foundation for various pottery and sculpture projects.

Terracotta Elephants

To create something that is big or heavy, the foundation, or legs should be strong. Otherwise the sculpture will tend to collapse.

Materials

Clay cylinders.

- Join two cylinders to form the front legs.

- Join two cylinders to form the back legs.

- Make a slab of clay to connect the two pairs of legs.

- Make a hollow sphere for the head and a cylinder for the trunk. Join them.

- Work slowly, adding another cylinder for the body.

- Complete the details of the elephant's features like eyes, ears, and tail, after smoothing out the rough edges.

Variation

- What other animals can one fashion with this technique?

SCULPTED HEADS

Solid structures made out of clay are heavy. They need to be small.

Materials

Clay, powder colours.

- Roll a ball of clay and form it into a head.

- Fill out details of the face by adding a nose.

- Hollow out the eyes and mouth.

- Allow it to dry, or if possible, fire it.

- Paint on details and features.

Variations

- To make it into a mobile, pierce a hole through the head before it dries. Suspend it from a string after it is dry.

Cylindrical Masks

A cylinder formed by glueing the ends of a sheet of paper is a simple way of turning a flat surface into a three-dimensional form. This can be the basis for creating objects like paper masks. They can be used in plays and performances.

Materials

Black chart paper, scissors, glue, white paint, brushes.

- Draw a face on the chart paper with white paint.

- Cut holes for the eyes, nose, and mouth.

- Fold the paper to form a cylinder and glue the edges.

PUPPETS

Forms evolve by simply filling up flat objects like paper covers.

Materials

Large brown paper cover, newspaper, black paper, poster paints, brushes, scissors, glue, string.

- Stuff the brown paper cover with crumpled newspaper and tie up the opening.

- What can be made of it? A face? An animal?

- Paint on features like eyes, nose, and mouth.

- Cut black paper strips for hair and glue them on.

- Try attaching a stick to the form to make a puppet.

- You can dress up the puppet with paper clothes.

Variation

- What other objects can you fill? Plastic bags? Old sacks?

LAYERS

Materials

Newspaper, black paper, scissors, glue.

- On a sheet of newspaper, outline the eyes, nose, and mouth of a face. Make small holes for the eyes. This is the first layer.

- Draw the same features on a sheet of black paper and cut out larger holes for the eyes, nose, and mouth. This is the second layer.

- Now draw the same features on another sheet of newspaper and cut out holes for them. These holes should be larger than those on the black paper. This is the third layer.

- Place layer 3 on layer 2, and layer 2 on layer 1.

- Glue the layers together.

- Fold the papers and glue the edges to form a cylindrical mask.

PAPER SCULPTURE

Paper glued on different moulds can serve as the basis on which to experiment with form.

Materials

Newspaper, glue, small flower pot, water.

- Wet the pot on the outside.

- Tear up newspaper into small pieces and wet them.

- Cover the pot with a layer of wet newspaper pieces.

- Apply glue over the wet paper and cover with another layer of wet newspaper.

- Repeat the process till you have a thick layer of newspaper, and allow it to dry.

- Separate the pot from the newspaper form.

COMBINATIONS & COMPOSITIONS

Combining different materials and media is a stimulating approach to compositions. Such combinations help to explore the different elements which go into making a composition: design, size and space. A good way of assembling compositions is through group work, where each child or adult can work on one element of the whole.

It is difficult to describe a good composition verbally. A sense of balance and harmony can be achieved by even a simple white line on black painted newspaper. The important thing is to know when and where to stop. Sometimes satisfying compositions can be created with minimum effort. Understanding, planning and organizing the elements in a picture leads to a harmonious composition.

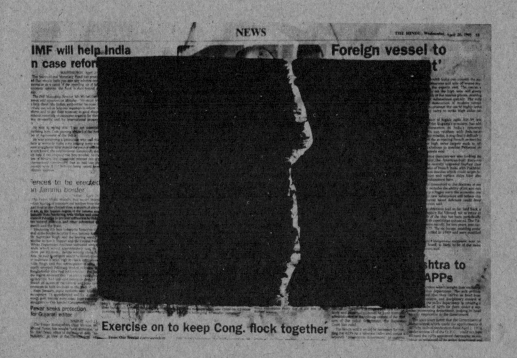

COLLAGE

Collages introduce composition to children who are reluctant to draw. You can develop a sense of form, colour and composition by focusing on a theme, and building on accidental forms.

Material

Sheet of black paper, bits of coloured paper, magazine sheets.

- Tear the magazine paper in to different sizes and shapes—which bits do you want to use as people, trees, houses, or rain?

- Place them on the black paper and move them around, until you are satisfied.

- Glue them on to the background.

- Add bits of coloured paper.

REVERSE ASSEMBLY

What goes into making a composition? To find out, create each of the elements in a picture separately and then assemble them.

Materials

White paper, crayons, felt pens, scissors, glue.

* Cut the white paper into small squares or rectangles.

* Think of a theme you would like to explore. Reflect on some of the things that go into making a picture related to your theme.

* Make these elements out of small pieces of paper and colour them. You can cut or tear them out.

* Arrange the elements on another sheet of paper and move them around until you are happy with the composition.

* Look at the background. Does it also need to be coloured? What about textures?

* Glue the different elements on to the background.

* Link them up with lines, to complete the composition.

Variation

* Try elements cut out of coloured paper.

MORE FROM MAGAZINES

Look at the possibilities that a sheet of magazine paper offers.
Observe the existing colours, tones, and textures. No two
people will 'see' the same thing. Your own interpretation will be
unique and original. Build on it.

Materials

Magazine paper, crayons

♦ Look at the texture of the print, the forms, and the colours in the
  paper. What do they suggest? How can they be developed?

♦ Add your own elements and colour with crayons.

Variation

♦ Try this exercise with newspaper instead of magazines.

Ghosts

Materials

Sheets of old faded black and brown paper, bright powder paints, glue, brushes.

- Place an old sheet of black paper on the floor, to form a background.

- Look at the discoloured paper to see if any 'forms' appear, to decide on a theme.

- Begin by outlining the forms with powder paints, filling in details like eyes, nose, hair, and mouth with colour.

- Draw clothes and hands on brown paper and cut them out.

- Glue these on to the background.

- Add further details with black paint.

Variation

- Try tearing the brown paper instead of cutting it.

This was a group effort involving eight children. It shows how faded waste paper can be used by looking closely at the tones in it and seeing what emerges from them.

Composing with Tones

Materials

Faded sheets of brown and black paper, black and white poster or powder paint, brushes, glue, board pins.

- Fasten four sheets of brown paper on to a big board with board pins, or lay them on the floor and glue the edges together to form a large background.

- Cut some circles out of black paper and glue them randomly over the brown paper surface. You can also cut animals or abstract shapes.

- With white paint, draw designs or complete facial features.

- Fill in additional details or shapes in black.

This mural was a group effort created for a drama workshop on the theme of youth and change.

Explorations & Transformations

Children enjoy playing with materials. If they start throwing clay around, use this to begin art work. Art originates in strange ways—from play and accidental discoveries, to new uses for everyday materials.

Often children are very disappointed when their work is 'spoiled' by an accident like a paint spill or finger prints. How does one create order out of chaos? Sometimes you are unhappy about the way your picture takes shape. Instead of throwing away such work, look at it again carefully, and give new life to it. It also helps to put away work with which you are dissatisfied, and look at it again later. It will appear different.

Spoilt Work

A child was unhappy with the finger prints he smeared on his picture of ducks. How could this be transformed? He made the smears into 'seeds' which his ducks could eat. Both the child and the ducks were happy!

Materials

Poster paints, brushes.

♦ Look at work which you think is 'spoilt'.

♦ Can you see any other form or figure in it? Can you work in the new form?

♦ With a brush and black paint outline the new shape you see.

♦ Integrate it into your work.

Magic Transfers

This striking print was the result of an accidental discovery. Clay was stored overnight, wrapped in newspaper, which got stuck to it. When the newspaper was peeled off the clay, a print remained on the clay surface.

Materials

Clay, newspaper.

- Form a slab of wet clay.

- Select the section of the newspaper you want printed and press it on to the clay slab.

- Allow it to dry.

- Carefully peel off the newspaper.

Variation

- Try other materials to generate prints.

Make Your Own Canvas

Materials

Paper, old cloth, raw rice powder, glue, water.

* Glue together several sheets of paper to get a thick sheet. You can also use thick chart paper.

* Apply glue on the paper, and stick the cloth onto it firmly.

* Make a paste with raw rice powder and water and spread it on the cloth surface. Allow it to dry.

* You can use any kind of paint on this 'canvas'.

Variation

* Try using a cloth-lined envelope as a base for your canvas.

NEWS PAPER

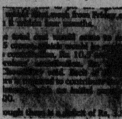

GADA CLOTH

BROWN PAPER

FLAT BRUSH   **GUM**

NEWSPAPER STICKS

This is a basic element, useful in many contexts. Children can arrange newspaper sticks into designs. They can be used as rods for puppets. Or they can form a doll theatre. These creations can even be glued on to a background and coloured.

Materials

Newspaper, glue, scissors.

+ Cut a square of newspaper.

+ Starting from one end of the square, roll the newspaper tightly to form a stick and glue it down firmly.

+ If you want a hollow stick, roll the newspaper tightly over a pencil. Then slide out the pencil and glue the newspaper down.

+ Make many sticks of varying thickness and length.

Variation

+ Try using magazine sheets and other coloured papers instead of newspaper.

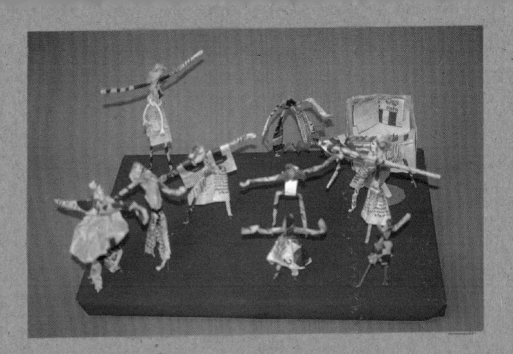

STAGE CRAFT

Materials

Newspaper sticks, scissors, glue, coloured paper, thermocole, toothpicks, stapler.

- Make puppets by glueing or stapling newspaper sticks together to form bodies, arms and legs.
- Dress them in clothes of your choice, made with bits of paper or chocolate wrappers.
- Arrange the figures on a thermocole sheet covered with coloured paper.
- To make them stand, insert toothpicks through their legs and pierce them into the thermocole sheet.

Variations

- What else can one do with such figures?
- They could be singers, dancers, or sports people.
- You could make a doll's house, or even a space station. You could also make furniture and other accessories.

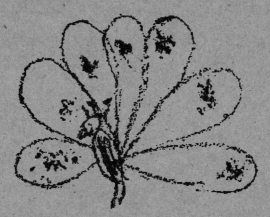

HOPSCOTCH

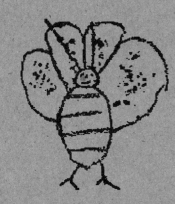

This was inspired by a simple children's game. Even very small children enjoy it. Bigger children can work with more details.

Materials

Paper, crayons or felt pens.

- Place your palm on the paper. Hop over your fingers with the other hand, marking dots and dashes with crayons or felt pens.

- You can sing a rhyme to it, in any language you know. You can also make your own rhyme.

- Remove your hand and look at the marks on the paper.

- Can you use these marks to form a composition?

- Put in details, and outline where necessary.

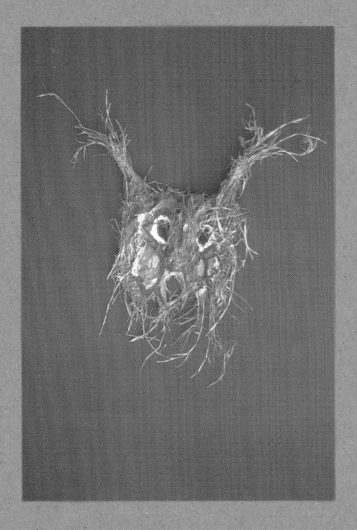

MUD AND STRAW

Dried grass and mud are typical art materials used by tribal communities.

Materials

Clay, straw or dried grass/hay, some bright poster or powder colour.

* Apply some mud on a layer of straw, so that it holds together.

* What does the form suggest? A mask? A human or animal face?

* Using coils of clay make the eyes, nose, mouth and other features.

* The straw can form the beard, mane or hair.

* Paint the features of the face with bright colours. Add designs.

* Display the straw masks on bright or black paper.

Variation

* Experiment with other natural materials like corn, leaves, sticks, or coconut husk.

Straw Horses

Straw is a very versatile material.

Materials

Straw, string, scissors.

- Tie up bunches of straw with string to make the body of the horse.

- Tie up another bunch to form the neck and face.

- With more straw, form the four legs and attach them to the body of the horse with string.

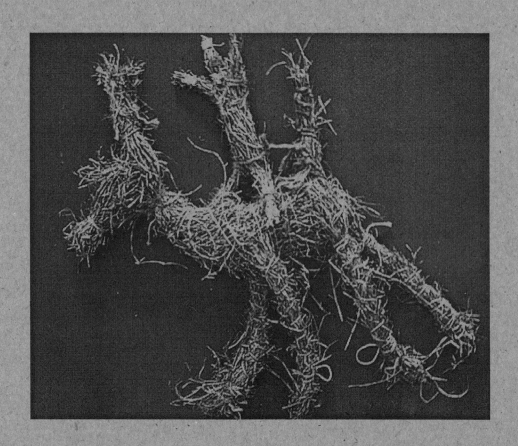

POT ART

Small clay flower pots turn very simply into mobiles and puppets.

Materials

Clay pot, string, poster or powder colours, brushes.

◆ Make two holes on the sides of the pot near the bottom.

◆ Thread a string through the holes to hang the pot upside down.

◆ Paint in a face with features and make it as decorative and colourful as you like.

Variation

◆ What else can a flower pot become?

CREATIVE DISPLAY

There should be no pressure for any kind of art work. Unfinished, spoilt, or broken work can be transformed by creative display.

Materials

White chart paper, unfinished or broken terracotta heads, string, black paint or felt pen, brushes.

- Pin up white paper onto an easel or board.

- Tie up the terracotta heads with string and suspend them from board pins onto the white paper.

- With a felt pen or black paint, outline the neck and body for each face on the white paper.

Variation

- What other compositions can you create? Can the terracotta pieces be worked into a different theme?

- Try glueing broken terracotta heads onto a background. Fill in details.

ALL YEAR ROUND

Creative art work can be put to practical use.

Materials

Small painting, cardboard, white or coloured paper, black felt pen, glue.

◆ Design a calendar for the current year on a sheet of white or coloured paper. You can even photocopy an existing calendar.

◆ Glue it onto the cardboard, leaving space for the picture.

◆ Glue the picture onto the cardboard.

S	M	T	W	T	F	S
1	2	3	4	5	6	7
8	9	10	11	12	13	14
15	16	17	18	19	20	21
22	23	24	25	26	27	28
29	30	31				

The art work in this book evolved out of explorations with children. Explore your own environment.

Even simple art work is effectively transformed by imaginative display. Display is essentially education and communication between the artist and the audience. Reflect on what is being displayed and how best to do it.

Generally, mounting art on some kind of background is effective. It helps if the background is not overpowering. Inexpensive brown paper looks earthy. Black paper can also be very effective.

Experiment with innovative display!

*Terracotta face
displayed against
a tree.*

CHILD ART WITH EVERYDAY MATERIALS

© 1996 Tara Publishing

Second printing 1998, this edition 2001

Art Concept: Tarit Bhattacharjee

Text: Kanchana Arni and Gita Wolf

Photographs: Helmut Wolf

Design: Deepa Kamath

Production: Saraswathi Ananth
and C. Arumugam

Tara Publishing
20/GA Shoreham, 5th Avenue
Chennai 600090, India
Ph: +91-44-4464479
Fax: +91-44-4911788
E-mail: tara@vsnl.com
www.tarabooks.com

ISBN 81-86211-17-9